World of Reptiles

Geckos

by Sally Velthaus

Consultants:
The Staff of Reptile Gardens
Rapid City, South Dakota

Capstone
press

Mankato, Minnesota

Bridgestone Books are published by Capstone Press,
151 Good Counsel Drive, P.O. Box 669, Mankato, Minnesota 56002.
www.capstonepress.com

Library of Congress Cataloging-in-Publication Data
Velthaus, Sally.
   Geckos / by Sally Velthaus.
     p. cm.—(Bridgestone Books. World of reptiles)
     Includes bibliographical references and index.
     ISBN 0-7368-4328-0 (hardcover)
   1. Geckos—Juvenile literature. I. Title. II. Series.
QL666.L245V45 2006
597.95'2—dc22   2004027944

Summary: A brief introduction to geckos, discussing their characteristics, range, habitat, food,
   offspring, and dangers. Includes a range map, life cycle diagram, and amazing facts.

Editorial Credits
Shari Joffe, editor; Enoch Peterson, set designer; Biner Design, book designer; Patricia Rasch, illustrator;
   Jo Miller, photo researcher; Scott Thoms, photo editor

Photo Credits
Bruce Coleman Inc./Erwin and Peggy Bauer, 16
Dwight R. Kuhn, 10
Michael Turco, cover, 4
Nature Picture Library/Anup Shah, 18
Pete Carmichael, 1, 6, 12
Tom Stack & Associates, Inc./Kitchin & Hurst, 20

1 2 3 4 5 6 10 09 08 07 06 05

Table of Contents

Geckos

Geckos get their name from the noise they make. It sounds like "gekko gekko."

Geckos are reptiles. Reptiles are **cold-blooded**. They can't make their own body heat. Reptiles also have scales and grow from eggs.

Geckos belong to a group of reptiles called lizards. Iguanas, monitors, and skinks are also lizards. More than 800 kinds of geckos live around the world.

◄ Geckos are the only lizards that have voices. They can make tiny barks, clicks, and squeaks.

What Geckos Look Like

Geckos have large heads and flat bodies. Their soft skin is covered with tiny scales that look like beads. Most geckos are less than 12 inches (30 centimeters) long.

A gecko can run across a ceiling without falling. The bottoms of its toes have pads covered with tiny hairs. These hairs can grab onto smooth surfaces. Geckos can even stick to glass.

Geckos have thick tails. The tail breaks off if a **predator** grabs it. The tail then grows back in a few months.

◀ Some geckos, like this day gecko, are brightly colored.

Gecko Range Map

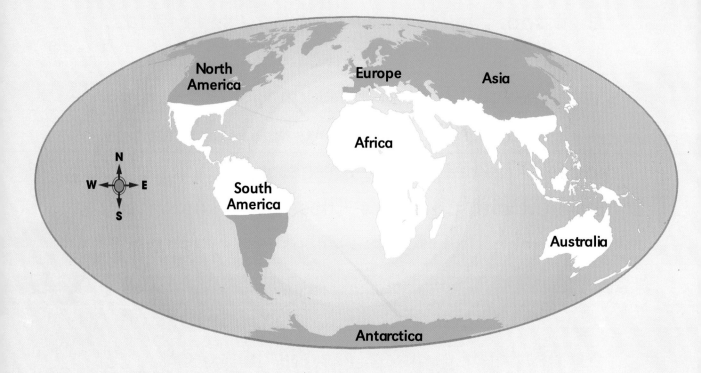

North America

Europe

Asia

Africa

South America

Australia

Antarctica

N
W · E
S

☐ Where Geckos Live

Geckos in the World

Geckos live in warm places throughout the world. They can be found on every continent except Antarctica. Australia has more than 100 kinds of geckos.

A few kinds of geckos live in the United States. Banded geckos are found in the Southwest. The leaf-toed gecko lives in California. Hawaii has many kinds of geckos.

Gecko Habitats

Geckos live in many **habitats**, including rain forests, deserts, and grasslands. Some geckos make their homes in mountains or canyons.

Geckos usually blend in with their surroundings. Leaves, branches, rocks, and sand are all hiding places for geckos. The leaf-tailed gecko lives in trees. The banded gecko hides in sand dunes. Most geckos hide during the day and come out at night.

◄ Geckos hide from predators by blending in with their habitats.

What Geckos Eat

Like many lizards, geckos eat insects and spiders. They hunt for their **prey** at night. People in many parts of the world like having geckos in their homes to catch bugs.

A few geckos eat other foods as well. Some geckos eat smaller geckos. Large geckos may eat small **mammals** such as mice. A few geckos eat fruit. A gecko that lives in New Zealand eats nectar from flowers.

Many kinds of geckos store fat in their tails. This fat helps them stay alive when they can't find food.

◄ This Tokay gecko has just caught a dragonfly.

The Life Cycle of a Gecko

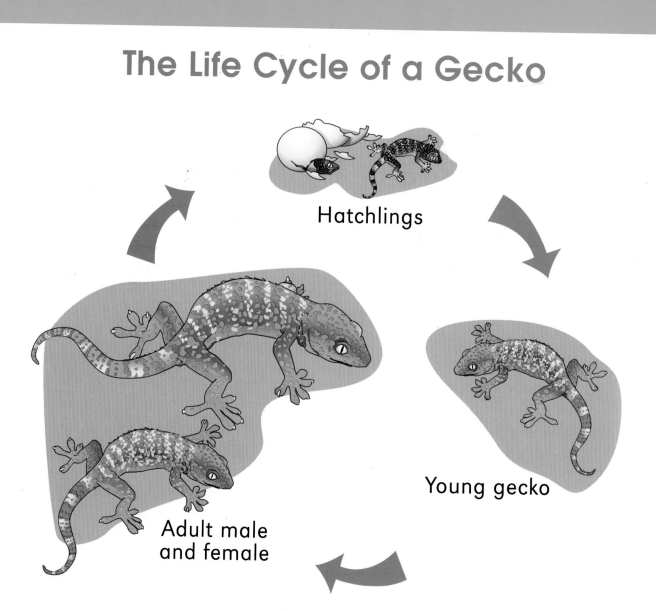

Hatchlings

Young gecko

Adult male
and female

Producing Young

Male and female geckos **mate** to produce eggs. Most female geckos lay two eggs at a time. The eggs are soft and white. The shells harden in the open air. Each set of eggs is called a **clutch**. Some geckos lay up to 10 clutches each year.

The mother lays the eggs under leaves or bark, where they can't be seen. The eggs hatch after about two months. Gecko hatchlings use a sharp tooth called an egg tooth to escape from their eggs.

Growing Up

Young geckos look like small adults. They live on their own as soon as they hatch. They hunt for food right away.

A gecko **molts**, or sheds its skin, as it grows. Some geckos eat the skin they shed.

Geckos that are cared for by people live about 5 to 10 years. Geckos in the wild live shorter lives.

◄ When a gecko molts, its skin breaks open at its head and falls off down its back.

Dangers to Geckos

Because geckos are small, they have many predators. Other lizards, snakes, and crocodiles hunt geckos. Birds, including eagles, also eat geckos. Spiders may eat the smallest geckos.

People are the biggest danger to geckos. They catch rare geckos to sell as pets. This practice leaves fewer geckos in the wild. People also destroy gecko habitats, especially forests. They clear land to build cities and towns. Even with these dangers, many geckos still live in the world.

◀ Agama lizards sometimes eat geckos.

Amazing Facts about Geckos

- Many kinds of geckos have no eyelids. These geckos sometimes use their tongues to clean their eyes.
- A gecko called the Jaragua lizard is the smallest lizard in the world. It is found in the Caribbean and can fit on a nickel.
- Flying geckos can glide. They have small flaps of skin on their heads, sides, feet, and tails. These flaps catch air as the gecko leaps from tree to tree.

◄ A gecko cleans its eye with its tongue.

Glossary

clutch (KLUHCH)—a group of eggs laid at one time

cold-blooded (KOHLD-BLUHD-id)—having a body temperature that is the same as its surroundings; all reptiles are cold-blooded.

habitat (HAB-uh-tat)—the place and natural conditions where an animal lives

mammal (MAM-uhl)—a warm-blooded animal that has a backbone; female mammals feed milk to their young.

mate (MAYT)—to join together to produce young

molt (MOHLT)—to shed an outer layer of skin

predator (PRED-uh-tur)—an animal that hunts other animals for food

prey (PRAY)—an animal hunted by another animal for food

Read More

Facklam, Margery. *Lizards: Weird and Wonderful.* New York: Little, Brown and Co., 2003.

Halfmann, Janet. *Lizards.* Nature's Predators. San Diego: Kidhaven Press, 2004.

Internet Sites

FactHound offers a safe, fun way to find Internet sites related to this book. All of the sites on FactHound have been researched by our staff.

Here's how:
1. Visit *www.facthound.com*
2. Type in this special code **0736843280** for age-appropriate sites. Or enter a search word related to this book for a more general search.
3. Click on the **Fetch It** button.

FactHound will fetch the best sites for you!

Index